Wild Ani

SLOTHS

GAIL TERP

BLACK RABBIT BOOKS

Bolt is published by Black Rabbit Books
P.O. Box 3263, Mankato, Minnesota, 56002.
www.blackrabbitbooks.com
Copyright © 2018 Black Rabbit Books

Jennifer Besel, editor; Grant Gould, interior designer; Michael Sellner, cover designer; Omay Ayres, photo researcher

All rights reserved. No part of this book may be reproduced, stored in a retrieval system or transmitted in any form or by any means, electronic, mechanical, photocopying, recording, or otherwise, without written permission from the publisher.

Library of Congress Cataloging-in-Publication Data
Terp, Gail, 1951- author.
Sloths / by Gail Terp. Wild animal kingdom.
Mankato, Minnesota : Black Rabbit Books, [2018] | Series: Bolt.
Wild animal kingdom | Audience: Ages 9-12. | Audience: Grades 4-6. | Includes bibliographical references and index.
Identifiers: LCCN 2016050032 (print) | LCCN 2016053542 (ebook) | ISBN 9781680721935 (library binding) | ISBN 9781680722574 (e-book) | ISBN 9781680724905 (paperback)
Subjects: LCSH: Sloths-Juvenile literature.
Classification: LCC QL737.E2 T47 2018 (print) | LCC QL737.E2 (ebook) | DDC 599.3/13-dc23
LC record available at https://lccn.loc.gov/2016050032

Printed in the United States at CG Book Printers,
North Mankato, Minnesota, 56003. 3/17

Image Credits

Alamy: Bill Hatcher, 28–29; blickwinkel/Hummel, 25 (eagle); blickwinkel/Lundqvist, 20 (swimming); Christian Ziegler / Danita Delimont, Agent, 17 (top); D. Hurst, 1, Back Cover; FLPA, 16–17; Gay Bumgarner, 23 (top); Glenn Bartley, 8–9; Island Road Images, 18; Ivan Kuzmin, 11; Dreamstime: Hotshotsworldwide, 6; Getty Images: Roy Toft, Cover; National Geographic Creative: JOEL SARTORE, 25 (sloth); Shutterstock: Airin.dizain, 14, 19 (left); Aleksey Stemmer, 25 (snake); Anan Kaewkhammul, 25 (jaguar); Beer5020, 26; COLOA Studio, 25 (leaves); Cuson, 4–5; Dennis Jacobsen, 23 (bottom); Elfred Tseng, 13; insima, 14–15; Kjersti Joergensen, 12; Kristel Segeren, 20 (full page); kungverylucky, 3; kzww, 25 (twigs); peruvianpictures.com, 22; Seaphotoart, 26–27; Volosina, 25 (flowers); zampe238, 32, ziinyn, 31
Every effort has been made to contact copyright holders for material reproduced in this book. Any omissions will be rectified in subsequent printings if notice is given to the publisher.

Contents

CHAPTER 1
A Day in the Life.....4

CHAPTER 2
Food to Eat and
a Place to Live.......10

CHAPTER 3
Family Life..........16

CHAPTER 4
Predators and
Other Threats........24

Other Resources............30

CHAPTER 1

A Day in the Life

A sloth hangs upside down in a tree. It slowly pulls a branch to its mouth. Its tough lips tear off a leaf. With peglike teeth, the sloth chews. It swallows and slowly reaches out again. It tears off a new leaf, chews, and swallows. The sloth does this again and again. Then, still hanging upside down, it sleeps. The sloth's claws keep a firm grip on the tree.

5

HOW BIG ARE SLOTHS?

three-toed sloth
16 TO 27 INCHES
(41 to 69 centimeters)
4 TO 15 POUNDS
(2 to 7 kilograms)

two-toed sloth
21 TO 29 INCHES
(53 to 74 cm)
11 TO 24 POUNDS
(5 to 11 kg)

Two Types

Sloths are amazing, and very slow-moving, animals. There are two families of sloths. Three-toed sloths have three toes on each foot. Two-toed sloths only have two toes on their front feet. They have three toes on their back feet.

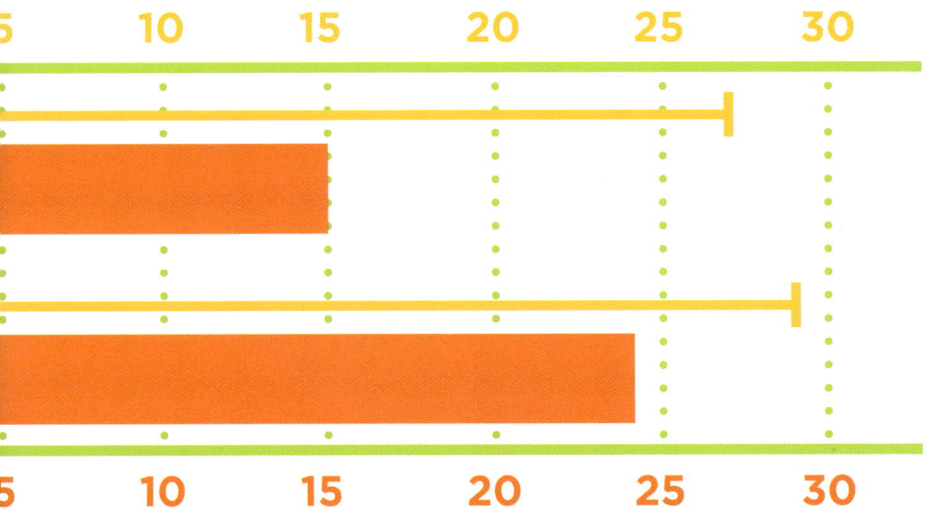

EARS

HEAD

SLOTH FEATURES

CLAWS

CHAPTER 2

Food to Eat
and a Place to Live

Sloths have a simple diet. They eat leaves, fruit, and soft twigs. Some eat flowers too. Their food provides most of their water. They also lick **dew** from leaves. Two-toed sloths feed only at night. Three-toed sloths feed day and night.

Sloths' hair is covered with green **algae**. The green color helps them blend in with the trees.

Slow Sloths

Sloths are rain forest animals. They live in Central and South America. They spend almost all their time in trees. In trees, sloths can move easily. But they don't move well on the ground. In fact, sloths can't even walk. Their **muscles** are too weak. They must pull themselves along the ground with their claws.

WHERE SLOTHS LIVE
Sloth Range Map

CHAPTER 3

Family Life

Sloths **mate** throughout the year. Most sloths have one baby at a time. Female sloths give birth in the trees. Some even give birth while upside down. Infants **nurse** for less than a month. Then they start to eat leaves. Adult males do not help care for the young.

Sloth hair is a home for insects. Ticks live there. Moths do too. Some moths lose their wings when they move in. These moths spend the rest of their lives in the hair.

COMPARING SIZES

18

Growing Up

Young sloths cling to their mothers' hair for up to a year. From there, they learn what food to eat. Within one year, the mothers leave their young. Like most sloths, the young will live alone.

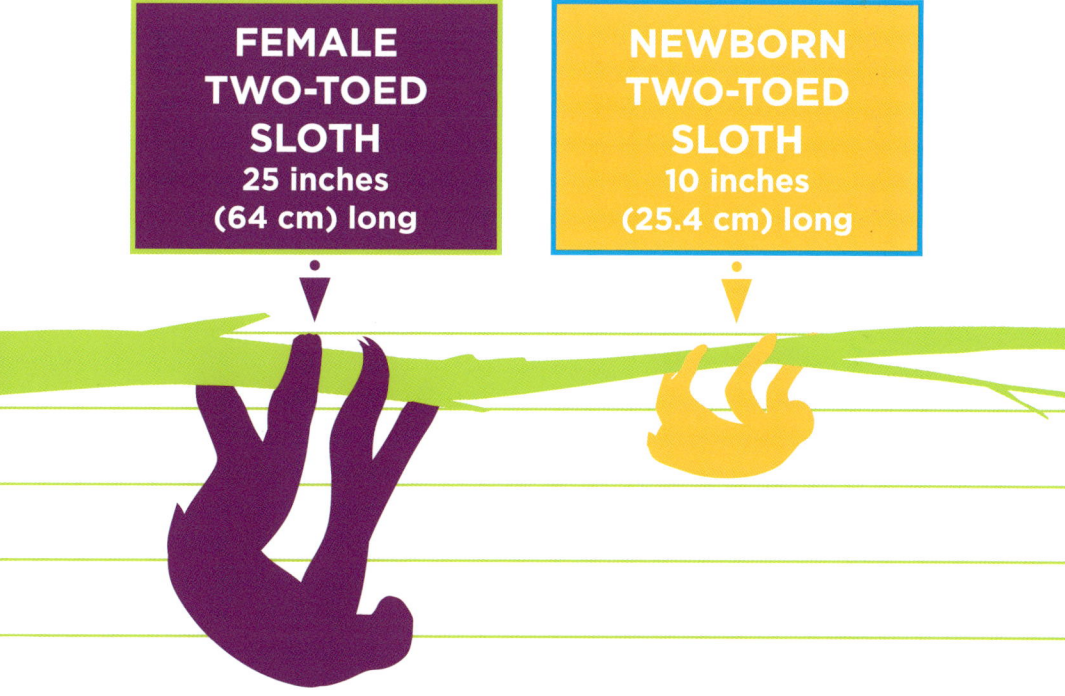

FEMALE TWO-TOED SLOTH
25 inches (64 cm) long
13 POUNDS (6 kg)

NEWBORN TWO-TOED SLOTH
10 inches (25.4 cm) long
.75 POUND (.3 kg)

Silent Sloths

Sloths are usually quiet. At times, mothers and their young will call to each other. Some sloths hiss when they're upset. But mostly, sloths are silent.

• •

Sloths are very good swimmers.

By the Numbers

6 to 8 FEET
(1.8 to 2.4 meters)
PER MINUTE

CLIMBING SPEED

NUMBER OF TEETH

18

about 30 YEARS
LIFE SPAN IN ZOOS

3 to 4 INCHES
(8 TO 10 CM)

LENGTH OF CLAWS

15 to 18 HOURS
HOW LONG SLOTHS SLEEP EACH DAY

CHAPTER 4

Predators
and Other Threats

Sloths have enemies. Wild cats, such as jaguars, **prey** on sloths. Eagles and snakes hunt them too. Sloths can't run from danger. But they will swipe their claws at enemies. Their sharp claws cut deeply.

Sloths and Humans

People cause problems for sloths. They cut down trees in the rain forest. Sloths have fewer trees to live in.

Humans also hunt sloths. Some people eat sloths. Others keep the animals as pets.

Protecting Sloths

People are working to protect sloths. They are trying to stop forests from being cut down. Then sloths can live safely.

Pygmy sloths are a type of three-toed sloth. They're **endangered**. Few pygmy sloths are left in the world. People are researching how to protect these creatures. With work, no type of sloth will be in danger.

All pygmy sloths live on one small island.

GLOSSARY

algae (AHL-jee)—any of a large group of simple plants and plantlike organisms that usually grow in water but do not produce seeds

dew (DOO)—drops of water that form outside at night on grass, trees, and other surfaces

endangered (in-DAYN-jurd)—close to becoming extinct

food chain (FOOD CHAYN)—a series of plants and animals in which each uses the next in the series as a food source

mate (MAYT)—to join together to produce young

muscle (MUH-suhl)—a body tissue that can contract and produce movement

nurse (NURS)—to feed a baby or young animal with milk from the mother's body

prey (PRAY)—to catch and eat something

LEARN MORE

BOOKS

Gregory, Josh. *Sloths.* Nature's Children. New York: Children's Press, an imprint of Scholastic Inc., 2016.

Lynette, Rachel. *Three-Toed Sloths.* Jungle Babies of the Amazon Rain Forest. New York: Bearport Publishing, 2013.

Murray, Julie. *Sloths.* I Like Animals! Minneapolis: Abdo Kids, 2017.

WEBSITES

Sloth
kids.nationalgeographic.com/animals/sloth/#sloth-beach-upside-down.jpg

Sloth Information And Facts For Kids
www.activewild.com/sloth-information-and-facts-for-kids/

Two-Toed Sloth
kids.sandiegozoo.org/animals/mammals/two-toed-sloth

INDEX

C
claws, 4, 8, 13, 23, 24

communication, 21

E
eating, 4, 10, 16, 19, 25

H
habitats, 4, 12, 13, 27, 28

hair, 9, 12, 17, 19

human threats, 27, 28

I
infants, 16, 18–19, 21

L
life spans, 23

P
predators, 24, 25, 27

R
ranges, 13, 14–15, 29

S
sizes, 6–7, 18–19

speeds, 4, 7, 22